TRIM
The Cartographer's Cat

The Ship's Cat Who Helped Flinders Map Australia

TRIM
The Cartographer's Cat

The Ship's Cat Who Helped Flinders Map Australia

Matthew Flinders, Philippa Sandall
and Gillian Dooley

Illustrations by Ad Long
Foreword by Julian Stockwin

**ADLARD
COLES**

LONDON • OXFORD • NEW YORK • NEW DELHI • SYDNEY

ADLARD COLES
Bloomsbury Publishing Plc
Kemp House, Chawley Park, Cumnor Hill, Oxford, OX2 9PH, UK

BLOOMSBURY, ADLARD COLES and the Adlard Coles logo are trademarks of
Bloomsbury Publishing Plc
First published in Great Britain 2019
Copyright © Philippa Sandall and Gillian Dooley, 2019

Illustrations © Ad Long, 2019

A catalogue record for this book is available from the British Library

Library of Congress Cataloguing-in-Publication data has been applied for

ISBN: HB: 978-1-4729-6722-0; ePub: 978-1-4729-6720-6; ePDF: 978-1-4729-6723-7

2 4 6 8 10 9 7 5 3 1

Typeset in Spectral Regular by Lee-May Lim
Printed and bound in China by Toppan Leefung Printing

FSC
www.fsc.org
MIX
Paper from
responsible sources
FSC® C104723

Dedication

To Lisette Flinders Petrie.
Thank you for sharing Trim's tale with the world.

Contents

Foreword
by Julian Stockwin

For some reason, the tale of Flinders and his much beloved cat has always touched me. Indeed, Trim's portrait resides proud and prominent in my writing cave as I write this.

My interest and respect actually goes back to my days serving in the Royal Australian Navy when I first learned about his vital role for the one who invented the term 'Australia'. In general, sea officers are not given to writing about their feelings and, as far as I'm aware, his epitaph and tribute to his cherished companion stands alone in history, giving us an all too human insight into what these feline shipmates meant to mariners confined to the boundaries of their so frail barks for months, even years at a time. He was clearly Flinders' cat, snuggling into his captain's cot, while on deck, tempests roared about them and always cheekily taking advantage of his quarterdeck status. At the same time, as is the way of the sea-cat, he would deign to walk and talk with the sailors, casting his beneficence without fear or favour both to high and low. Even, to my considerable admiration and esteem, swarming up the ratlines to join them in the main-top in fisting the sails to a reef – albeit in a supervisory capacity.

At sea, the captain of a ship is in a peculiar situation. The merchant service has a quaint phrase to be found in the ship's papers which, for me, sums it up in one: he is 'Master under God' of his particular ship. Every soul aboard must render him respect and obedience, but in return, they could place their complete trust in him to see them through life and death perils of a kind never to be faced on land. There was no-one the captain himself could share his fears and doubts with and all decisions must be his own.

The 'loneliness of command' was and is a very real thing for the captain of a ship but how much more was it for a solitary explorer of unutterably remote regions whose only maps and charts were the ones he made up himself as he sailed ever deeper into the vast unknown? That Flinders knew he was all but forgotten while the rest of the world was locked into a bitter war for survival and supremacy could only intensify his feelings, and that Trim was there to share them was, from the evidence in this volume, crucial to the success of this epic of navigation.

And that the pen of Philippa Sandall, the original Seafurrer, should be the one to bring this saga together can only be meet and right!

Julian Stockwin, an avowed cat lover himself, writes the internationally-acclaimed *Thomas Kydd* series of historical adventure fiction. More information can be found on his website www.julianstockwin.com

Introduction

While many of us have grieved over the loss of a beloved pet, few of us have turned our sadness into a tribute, let alone a tribute that's become the world's most timeless tale about a ship's cat.

Matthew Flinders did. While the manuscript found among his papers is dated 1809, he was clearly rehearsing this story in his heart and head for some time as there were at least two earlier drafts in English and French. 'Translating into French the history of my cat Trim, which I wrote out for the purpose,' he notes in his Private Journal on Sunday 11 January 1807.

It's not hard to imagine Flinders, while stuck in Mauritius, enlivening the lessons he gave Madame Louise d'Arifat's children in mathematics, principles of navigation and English with tales of Trim's intrepid adventures. Nor is it hard to imagine him heading home and putting pen to paper, egged on by their delighted response and requests for more. The story he has left us is more than a story about a ship's cat who lapped and mapped Australia, it's a story packed with informal details of shipboard life you won't find in logs or official accounts of voyages.

From the very first lines, Flinders sets a light-hearted tone, renaming HMS *Investigator* the *Spyall* because investigating is a kind of 'spying'; *Reliance* he renamed the *Roundabout* because

she made numerous roundabout trips to Norfolk Island. Later, the *Porpoise* becomes the *Janty*, which means 'jaunty', which the *Porpoise* absolutely wasn't; and the *Cumberland* becomes the *Minikin*, which means small and insignificant, which *Cumberland* absolutely was – 'something less than a Gravesend Package Boat', according to Flinders.

For *Trim, The Cartographer's Cat*, we went back to Flinders' manuscript. As the original is safely lodged in the National Maritime Museum at Greenwich, we contented ourselves with the PDF they supplied to make a complete and faithful new transcript, correcting the many little errors we have found in various online and print editions, some of which are also significantly abridged. The *Tribute* manuscript is a six-page booklet, and it is so remarkable, we have included an excerpt (on page 51) so that readers can share our awe at Flinders' beautiful handwriting and straight lines. While we have retained his spelling, punctuation and paragraph breaks, we have corrected the odd typo such as a missing full stop – Matthew didn't have the advantage of a proofreader. We have also italicised the names of ships for editorial consistency throughout.

We have also added 'friendly footnotes' * to provide some

A Biographical Tribute

to the memory

of Trim.

Isle of France, Dec.

1809

background to his literary allusions (Flinders was very well read) and the nautical terms that might mystify modern-day and non-nautical readers.

To give readers a picture of Trim's life and times, we turned to the treasure trove of material created on the *Investigator* during the circumnavigation of Australia, in the form of the drawings of William Westall and Ferdinand Bauer.

Although we will never know, it's reasonable to assume that *A Biographical Tribute to the Memory of Trim* would not have been written if Flinders had not been detained in Mauritius by the Governor, General Decaen. His plan was to hotfoot it back to London, get himself a new ship and complete charting Australia's coastline with Trim at his side. That's why we have included Gillian's short essay on where Flinders was when he wrote the *Tribute* and why, and what his letters and journals from that time tell us about his 'sporting, affectionate and useful companion'.

What were Trim's views on all this? In 'My Seafurring Adventures with Matt Flinders', Trim uses snippets from the *Tribute* as a springboard to add some background to what he saw as a premature Epitaph, as well as fill in gaps and, on occasion, set the record straight. He modestly confesses that he didn't complete this memoir entirely on his own, roping in the services of a couple of scribes to help him pull it all together.

A Biographical Tribute to the Memory of Trim

**Matthew Flinders RN
Cartographer**

Isle of France
Dec. 1809

I can never speak of cats without a sentiment of regret for my poor Trim, the favourite of all our ship's company on the *Spyall*. This good-natured purring animal was born on board His Majesty's ship the *Roundabout* in 1799 during a passage from the Cape of Good Hope to Botany Bay; and saving the rights and titles of the Parish of Stepney,* was consequently an Indian by birth. The signs of superior intelligence which marked his infancy procured for him an education beyond what is usually bestowed upon the individuals of his tribe; and being brought up amongst sailors, his manners acquired a peculiarity of cast which rendered them as different from those of other cats, as the actions of a fearless seaman are from those of a lounging, shame-faced ploughboy; it was, however, from his gentleness and the innate goodness of his heart, that I gave him the name of my uncle Toby's honest, kind-hearted, humble companion.†

In playing with his little brothers and sisters upon deck by moon-light, when the ship was lying tranquilly in harbour, the energy and elasticity of his movements sometimes carried him so far beyond his mark, that he fell overboard; but this was far from being a misfortune; he learned to swim and to have no dread of the water; and when a rope was thrown over to him, he took hold

---

* The rights and titles of the parish of Stepney were the English registers of births, marriages and deaths from 1538 to 1815.
† 'Uncle Toby's honest, kind-hearted, humble companion' was Corporal Trim in Laurence Sterne's novel *Tristram Shandy* (published in nine volumes from 1759 to 1767).

of it like a man, and ran up by it like a cat; in a short time, he was able to mount up the gangway steps quicker than his master, or even than the first lieutenant.

Being a favourite with everybody on board, both officers and seamen, he was well fed, and grew fast both in size and comeliness; a description of his person will not be misplaced here. From the care that was taken of him, and the force of his own constitution, Trim grew to be one of the finest animals I ever saw; his size even emulated that of his friends of Angora:* his weight being from ten to twelve pounds according as our fresh-meatometer stood high or low. His tail was long, large and bushy; and when he was animated by the presence of a stranger of the anti-catean race, it bristled out to a fearful size, whilst vivid flashes darted from his fiery eyes, though at other times he was candour and good nature itself. His head was small and round, – his physionomy bespoke intelligence and confidence, – wiskers long and graceful, – and his ears were cropped in a beautiful curve. Trim's robe was a clear jet black, with the exception of his four feet, which seemed to have been dipped in snow; and his under lip, which rivalled them in whiteness; he had also a white star on his breast, and it seemed as if nature had designed him for the prince and model of his race:

---

* Angora cats, originally from Ankara in central Turkey, were popular pets in eighteenth-century Europe – Marie-Antoinette had six who, the story goes, escaped the guillotine and emigrated to America.

I doubt whether Whittington's cat, of which so much has been said and written, was to be compared to him.*

Notwithstanding my great partiality to my friend Trim, strict justice obliges me to cite in this place a trait in his character which by many will be thought a blemish; he was, I am sorry to say it, excessively vain of his person, particularly of his snow-white feet. He would frequently place himself on the quarter deck before the officers, in the middle of their walk; and spreading out his two white hands in the posture of the lion couchant, oblige them to stop and admire him. They would indeed say low to each other, "See the vanity of that cat"! But they could not help admiring his graceful form and beautiful white feet. Indeed when it is known, that to the finest form ever beheld, he joined extraordinary personal and mental qualifications, the impossibility that the officers could be angry with him must be evident; and they were men of too much elevation of mind to be jealous of him. I would not be an advocate in the cause of vanity; but if it is ever excusable, it was so in this case. How many men are there, who have no claim either from birth, fortune, or acquirements, personal or mental,

---

* While Dick Whittington's cat starred in ballads, plays, pantomimes and puppet shows, there's no evidence the Lord Mayor of London ever had a cat.

whose vanity is not to be confined within such harmless bounds, as was that of Trim! And I will say for him, that he never spoke ill of, or objected to the pretensions of others, which is more than can be said for very many bipeds.

... who's the fairest
of them all?

Trim, though vain as we have seen, was not like those young men who, being assured of an independence, spend their youth in idle trifling, and consider all serious application as pedantic and derogatory, or at least to be useless; he was, on the contrary, animated with a noble zeal for the improvement of his faculties. His exercises commenced with acquiring the art of leaping over the hands; and as every man in the ship took pleasure in instructing him, he at length arrived to such a pitch of perfection, that I am persuaded, had nature placed him in the empire of Lilliput*, his merit would have promoted him to the first offices in the state.

He was taught to lie flat upon the deck on his back, with his four feet stretched out like one dead; and in this posture he would remain until a signal was given him to rise, whilst his preceptor resumed his walk backwards and forwards; if, however, he was kept in this position, which it must be confessed was not very agreeable to a quadruped, a slight motion of the end of his tail denoted the commencement of impatience, and his friends never pushed their lessons further.

Trim took a fancy to learning nautical astronomy. When an officer took lunar or other observations, he would place himself by the time-keeper, and consider the motion of the hands, and

* Lilliput is the fictional island in Jonathan Swift's *Gulliver's Travels* (1726) which was ruled over by an emperor and inhabited by very small people, who were roughly the size of Trim.

apparently the uses of the instrument, with much earnest attention; he would try to touch the second hand, listen to the ticking, and walk all round the piece to assure himself whether or no it might not be a living animal; and mewing to the young gentleman whose business it was to mark down the time, seemed to ask an explanation.* When the officer had made his observation, the cry of Stop! roused Trim from his meditations; he cocked his tail, and running up the rigging near to the officer, mewed to know the meaning of all those proceedings. Finding at length that nature had not designed him for an astronomer, Trim had too much good sense to continue a useless pursuit; but a musket ball slung with a piece of twine, and made to whirl round upon the deck by a slight motion of the finger, never failed to attract his notice, and to give him pleasure; perhaps from bearing a near resemblance to the movement of his favourite planet the moon, in her orbit around the primary which we inhabit.

---

* The ticking time-keeper that engaged Trim's earnest attention was the marine chronometer used to determine longitude at sea. It was invented by one of Lincolnshire's famous sons, John Harrison. Flinders, another of Lincolnshire's famous sons, had five time-keepers on the *Investigator*, and he had a favourite one – Thomas Earnshaw's E520. 'This excellent time-keeper,' he called it. He had E520 with him when he was detained in Port Louis in 1803, and gave it to Mr Aken, master of the *Investigator*, to take back to England when he was released in 1810. 'E520 has been delivered to the Greenwich Observatory,' announced the Astronomer Royal, Neville Maskelyne, to the Board of Longitude on 12 December that year. It now resides in the Museum of Applied Arts and Sciences in Sydney.

He was equally fond of making experiments upon projectile forces and the power of gravity; if a ball was thrown gently along the deck, he would pursue it; and when the gravitating principle combined with the friction overcame the impelling power, he would give the ball a fresh impetus, but generally to turn its direction into an elliptic curve; at other times the form of the earth appeared to be the object of his experiments, and his ball was made to describe an oblate spheroid. The seamen took advantage of this his propensity to making experiments with globular bodies; and two of them would often place themselves, one at each end of the forecastle, and trundling a ball backwards and forwards from one to the other, would keep Trim in constant action running after it; his admiration of the planetary system having induced an habitual passion for everything round that was in motion. Could Trim have had the benefit of an Orrery, or even of being present at Mr. Walker's experiments in natural philosophy,* there can be no doubt as to the progress he would have made in the sublimest of sciences.

---

* Adam Walker (1731–1821) built an 'eidouranion' (a large transparent 'orrery', or mechanical model of the solar system with back projection) measuring 27 feet in diameter to provide his renowned astronomical lecture demonstrations with dazzling stage effects. It was accompanied by the other-worldly tones of a 'celestina', the glass organ that he had patented on 29 July 1772, and audiences at places like the Royal Theatre and the Lyceum Theatre in London were enthralled.

The greatest discoveries are sometimes due to accident. It must now be evident, that some celebrated cat of antiquity, perhaps one of those which entered with Noah into the ark and from which Trim was probably a descendant, gave rise, by the great profundity of his meditations, to the personification of wisdom adopted in the hyeroglyphic paintings and sculptures of the first ages. When afterwards Minerva was made the emblem of wisdom, she was long accompanied by a cat, to mark the attribute she represented; and with all deference to the F.A.Ses, I presume to conjecture, that it was not until about the time of Pericles, when all the divine attributes were made to take a human form, that this Grecian divinity could dispense with the presence of her companion. It was not the presence of Minerva which shewed the cat to be the personification of the wisdom of the great Jao-Πατηρ or Jupiter, but that of the cat which explained what Minerva was intended to represent. I could go still further, and shew, that by a simple transformation of all the letters [illegible – 'Sofia'?] (wisdom), and [illegible – 'Felis'?] (cat, domestic happiness) have the same etimological root; or are rather identically the same word. It would be worth enquiring to know whether this holds good in the Cophtic, Phenician, and Chinese languages.*

---

* While Flinders may be tacking down the wrong classical track, sorting out mythology's 'Who's Who' can be challenging. Not even the F.A.Ses (Fellows of the Society of Antiquaries) got it right all the time. The 'divinity' from antiquity unquestionably associated with the cat is Egypt's Bastet. As Bast, she was originally a maned lion goddess, revered for her ferocity, but she was later transformed into the adored household favourite and goddess of fertility, Bastet – female cats were noted for their fecundity. When the Greeks discovered her, they called her ailuros (Greek for 'cat') and, since cats weren't household favourites in Greece, likened her to Artemis, their goddess of hunting and wild animals (Diana is the Roman equivalent). No wisdom or owls. However, in Classical Cats, Professor Donald Engels says some Greek sources (he doesn't specify which) state that the cat was sacred to Athena Glaukopis (Athena of the Shining Eyes), and her Roman equivalent is Minerva, the wise one with an owl on her wrist. Challenging.

His desire to gain a competent knowledge in practical seamanship, was not less than he shewed for experimental philosophy. The replacing a top-mast carried away, or taking a reef in the sails, were what most attracted his attention at sea; and at all times when there was more bustle upon deck than usual, he never failed to be present and in the midst of it; for as I have before hinted, he was endowed with an unusual degree of confidence and courage, and having never received anything but good from men, he believed all to be his friends, and he was the friend of all. When the nature of the bustle upon the deck was not understood by him, he would mew and rub his back up against the legs of one and the other, frequently at the risk of being trampled under foot, until he obtained the attention of someone to satisfy him. He knew what good discipline required, and on taking in a reef, never presumed to go aloft until the order was issued; but so soon as the officer had given the word – "Away up aloft!"; up he jumped along with the seamen; and so active and zealous was he, that none could reach the top before, or so soon as he did. His zeal, however, never carried him beyond a sense of his dignity: he did not lay out on the yard like a common seaman, but always remained seated upon the cap, to inspect like an officer. This assumption of authority to which, it must be confessed, his rank, though great as a quadruped, did not entitle him amongst men, created no jealousy; for he always found some good friend ready to caress him after the business was done, and to take him down in his arms.

In harbour, the measuring of log and lead lines upon deck, and the stowage of the holds below, were the favourite subjects of his attention. No sooner was a cask moved, than he darted in under it upon the enemies of his king and country, at the imminent risk of having his head crushed to atoms, which he several times very narrowly escaped. In the bread room he was still more indefatigable; he frequently solicited to be left there alone and in the dark, for two or three days together, that nothing might interrupt him in the discharge of his duty. This is one of the brightest traits in my friend Trim's character, and would indeed do honour to any character; in making the following deductions from it I shall not, I think, be accused of an unjust partiality. 1st. it must be evident that he had no fear of evil spirits; and consequently that he had a conscience above reproach. 2nd; it is clear that he possessed a degree of patience and perseverance, of which few men can boast; and 3rd. that like a faithful subject, he employed all these estimable qualities in the service of His Majesty's faithful servants, and indirectly of His Majesty himself. Alas! my poor Trim; thy extraordinary merit required only to be known, in order to excite universal admiration.

Trim was admitted upon the table of almost every officer and man in the ship; in the gunroom* he was always the first ready for dinner; but though he was commonly seated a quarter of an hour before any other person, his modest reserve was such that his voice was not heard until everybody else was served. He then put in his request, not for a full allowance, he was too modest – nor did he desire there should be laid for him a plate, knife, fork, or spoon, with all which he could very well dispense; – but by a gentle caressing mew, he petitioned for a little, little bit, a kind of tythe from the plate of each; and it was to no purpose to refuse it, for Trim was enterprising in time of need, as he was gentle and well bred in ordinary times. Without the greatest attention to each morsel, in the person whom he had petitioned in vain; he would whip it off the fork with his paw, on its passage to the mouth, with such dexterity and an air so graceful, that it rather excited admiration than anger. He did not, however, leap off the table with his prize, as if he had done wrong; but putting the morsel into his mouth and eating it quietly, would go to the next person and repeat his little mew: if refused his wonted tythe, he stood ready to take all advantages. There are some men so inconsiderate

* Flinders and Trim dined in the gunroom, the junior officers' mess (for officers below the rank of lieutenant) on the Cape Town to Botany Bay voyage. In January 1798, Flinders obtained his lieutenant's commission, and he and Trim moved up to the wardroom, where the commissioned naval officers ate.

as to be talking when they should be eating, – who keep their meat suspended in mid-air till a semi-colon in the discourse gives an opportunity of taking their mouthful without interrupting their story. Guests of this description were a dead mark for Trim: when a short pause left them time to take the prepared mouthful, they were often surprised to find their meat gone, they could not tell how.

Trim had one day missed a fine morsel from the hungry activity of one of the young gentlemen (the present captain D.) who dined in the gunroom; seeing him, however, talking and eating at the same time, my persevering gentleman did not give it up, though the piece was half masticated and only waited for a period to disappear; but running up the waistcoat of our unsuspecting guest, for Trim was then but a kitten, and placing one paw at each corner of his mouth, he laid vigourous siege to his morsel; and whilst the astonished midshipman inarticulately exclaimed, G..d d...n the cat! Trim fairly took the piece out of his mouth and carried it off. This was pushing his enterprises too far, and he therefore received a reprimand which prevented them in future.

The gunroom steward was, however, more particularly Trim's confidant; and though he had dined with the masters, he was not too proud to sit down a second time with the servant. William had such an opinion of Trim's intelligence, that he talked to him as to his child, whilst my four-footed master looking up in his face, seemed to understand him and to give rational answers. They had the following conversation after dinner on the day of Trim's audacious enterprise just related.

Do you know, master Trim, that you have behaved very ill? – Me-ew?

It is very well to play your tricks with those that know you, but you should be more modest with strangers. – Mew!

How dare you say that I gave you no breakfast? Did I not give you all the milk that was left, and some bread soaked in it? – Mou – wow!*

No meat! What! you grow insolent? I'll chain you up; do you hear Sir? – Me-ew.

Well, if you'll promise to behave better, you shall have a nice piece off the cold shank of mutton for your supper, you shall. – Mew – wew!!

Gently master Trim. I'll give it you now, but first promise me upon your honour. – Me-wee.

Come then my good boy, come up and kiss me.

Trim leaped up on his shoulder, and rubbing his face up against William's cheek, received the mutton, piece by piece out of his mouth.

---

* Trim enjoyed officer privileges such as fresh milk and fresh mutton at mealtimes. No salt beef for those dining in the gunroom or the wardroom. At the start of a voyage, navy ships often sounded and smelled like a farmyard, with animals stowed in odd corners of the decks to provide fresh food for the officers. Not all were eaten. Seaman George Watson, remembering life on board HMS *Fame*, wrote in his *Narrative of the Adventures of a Greenwich Pensioner*: "We had live stock on board of every kind, in abundance: bullocks, pigs, sheep, goats, geese, ducks, turkeys, chickens &c; many of these creatures becoming domesticated, were spared the general slaughter, and had names given to them by the Tars, there was Billy the goat; Jenny the cow; Tom, the sheep; Jack, the goose; and many others, which I shall not mention; Jenny the cow, after being two years on board, ran dry, and therefore, was killed … poor Tom the sheep was killed by lightning."

In an expedition made to examine the northern parts of the coast of New South Wales, Trim presented a request to be of the party, promising to take upon himself the defence of our bread bags, and his services were accepted. Bongaree,* an intelligent native of Port Jackson, was also on board our little sloop; and with Trim formed an intimate acquaintance. If he had occasion to drink, he mewed to Bongaree and leaped up to the water cask; if to eat, he called him down below and went strait to his kid,† where there was generally a remnant of black swan. In short, Bongaree was his great resource, and his kindness was repaid with caresses. In times of danger, Trim never shewed any signs of fear; and it may truly be said, that he never distrusted or was afraid of any man.

---

* Bongaree (Bungaree, c.1775–1830) was the first Aboriginal to circumnavigate mainland Australia as far as we know. He was possibly more familiar with Australia's coastline than anyone else at the time, since he had taken part in more voyages of exploration than anyone else. He dipped his exploration toe in the water with Henry Waterhouse in the *Reliance* on a round trip to Norfolk Island in 1798. Then he sailed with Flinders in the *Norfolk* in 1799 to examine the northern parts of the coast of New South Wales, and in the *Investigator* 'to explore the whole of the coasts' of New Holland (1802–03); with James Grant in the *Lady Nelson* to Port Macquarie (1804); and with Phillip Parker King in the *Mermaid* to survey Northwest Cape and Arnhem Land (1817).

† A 'kid' is a small wooden tub for grog or rations.

Portrait of Bungaree, a native of New South Wales, with Fort Macquarie, Sydney Harbour, in background, Augustus Earle. Oil on canvas c.1826. National Library of Australia.

In 1800, the *Roundabout* returned to England by the way of Cape Horn and St. Helena, and thus Trim, besides his other voyages, completed the tour of the globe. Many and curious are the observations which he made in various branches of science, particularly in the natural history of small quadrupeds, birds, and flying fish, for which he had much taste. These, with his remarks upon men and manners, if future leisure should enable me to put them into order, I may perhaps give to the world; and from the various seas and countries he has visited, joined to his superior powers for distinguishing obscure subjects, and talents for seizing them, these observations may be expected to be more interesting than the imaginary adventures of your guineas, shillings, or half-pence, and to possess more originality than the Turkish spy.*

* In the *Tribute*, Flinders includes numerous references to books that were popular reading at the time. Joseph Addison's essay 'Adventures of a Shilling' refers to 'imaginary adventures of your guineas, shillings, or half-pence', while the Turkish spy is a nod to *Letters Writ by a Turkish Spy*. This was an eight-volume (fictional) collection of letters by Mahmut, an Ottoman spy at Louis XIV's court, probably penned by Giovanni Paolo Marana, then translated into English, and running through fifteen editions by 1801.

Trim was not alone in developing a taste for flying fish. Seafarers have long welcomed their Uber Eats plopping-down-on-deck habit. However, flying is a bit of a misnomer says fish expert Frank Fish. They are actually gliding using their pectoral and pelvic fins as wings. 'To take off a fish leaps from the water or rises to the surface continually beating its tail to generate propulsion as it starts to taxi. The taxiing run lets the fish accelerate at water surface and build momentum for take-off. Once the fish reaches its top speed of 20 to 40 miles an hour (32 to 64 kilometres per hour) it spreads its elongate fins and becomes airborne, gliding for 50 to 100 feet (15 to 30 metres).'

Flying Fish. Exocoetus sp. Ferdinand Bauer. Natural History Museum.

Trim was not only a stranger to England, but also to a house and to the manner of living in it. The king of Bantam's ambassador* was not more inexperienced in these matters than he. I took a lodging for him at Deptford, placing him under the guardianship of the good woman of the house, who promised to instruct him in the usages of Terra firma; but she knew not what she had undertaken. He would go out at the sash window to the top of the house, for the convenience of making his observations on the surrounding country more at ease; – it came on to rain, – the sash was put down. This would have been an invincible obstacle to other cats, but not so to Trim: he bolted through the glass like a clap of thunder, to the great alarm of the good hostess below. "Good God, Trim," exclaimed she on entering the chamber, "is it thee? They said thou wast a strange outlandish cat, and verily I think thou art the divil: I must shut thee up, for if thou go'st to treat neighbours thus, I shall have thee taken up for a burglary. But come, I know thy master will pay the damage: hast thou cut thyself?"

---

* 'There was more than one ambassador from Bantam. Eight arrived in London on 28 April 1682 and were received by the King at Windsor. Bantam was a major trading centre for pepper and other spices; silks and porcelain from China; scented woods and Indian textiles. The East India Company had a factory there. The most likely source for this reference is James Granger's *Biographical History of England from Egbert the Great to the Revolution* (1769), a book that Flinders' father probably had on his shelves.

TRIM'S
    SHORT CUT
GLASS ALL SMASHED TO "FLINDERS".

Trim's short cut, glass all smashed to 'Flinders', George Gordon McCrae. National Library of Australia. George Gordon McCrae probably dashed off this sketch while researching and writing about Flinders. He had access to Flinders' papers in Australia, including those William Matthew Flinders Petrie copied and presented to McCrae's friend, John Joseph Shillinglaw, who was collecting material for a book on Flinders. McCrae may well have been the first person in Australia to read Flinders' *Tribute to Trim*; he was certainly the first to illustrate it. Shillinglaw gave many of the papers he acquired to the State Library of Victoria, but the *Tribute* does not seem to be among them – tracking down its movements would be a nice little research project for a keen archivist.

Woe to the good woman's china, if Trim got into her closet. Your delicat town-bred cats go mincing in amongst cup and saucers without touching them; but Trim! If he spied a mouse there he dashed at it like a man of war, through thick and thin: the splinters flew in all directions. The poor woman at first thought an evil spirit was playing his pranks in her cupboard; – she opens the door with fear and trembling; when, to her infinite dismay, out jumps my black gentleman upon her shoulder: she was well nigh dead with fear. Seeing how much mischief was done to her dear china, the pride of her heart, she seized Trim to beat him soundly; but instead of trying to escape, the droll animal rubs his wiskers up against her chin and falls to purring. She had no longer the heart to strike him; but after a moment's hesitation, she heaved a sigh and picked up the pieces.

I took him up to London in the stage coach, and as there were no fine ladies to be frightened at the presence of a strange cat, he was left at full liberty. He was not in the least disconcerted by the novelty of his situation; but placing himself upon the seat, and stretching out his white paws, conducted himself reasonably like any other passenger, to the admiration of two gentlemen who did not cease to make inquiries concerning his education, manners, and adventures, during the whole way to town.

A worthy acquaintance in London took Trim into his family; but he soon requested me to take him back, for "such a strange animal," said he, "I never saw. I am afraid of losing him. He goes out into the streets in the middle of the day, and rubs himself against the legs of people passing by. Several have taken him up to caress him, but I fear some one will be carrying him off." I took him on board the *Spyall* to make a second voyage to the South Seas.* Trim now found himself at home; and his gentleness and extraordinary confidence, joined to the amusement his droll antics furnished them, soon made him as great a favourite with his new shipmates, as he had been on board the *Roundabout*. We had several dogs on board the *Spyall*, but Trim was undisputed master of them all. When they were at play upon the deck, he would go in amongst them with his stately air; and giving a blow at the eyes of one, and a scratch on the nose to another, oblige them to stand out of his way. He was capable of being animated against a dog, as dogs usually may be against a cat; and I have more than once sent him from the quarter deck to drive a dog off the forecastle. He would run half the way briskly, crouching like a lion which has prey in view; but then assuming a majestic deportment, and without being deterred by the menacing attitude of his opponent, he would march straight up to him, and give him a blow on the nose, accompanied with a threatening mew! If the dog did not immediately retreat, he flew at him with his war cry of Yow! If resistance was still made, he leaped up on the rail over

---

* On 19 January 1801, a commission was signed at the Admiralty appointing Flinders lieutenant of His Majesty's Sloop *Investigator (Spyall)*.

View in Sir Edward Pellew's group, Gulph [sic] of Carpentaria, William Westall; engraved by John Pye. National Library of Australia.

his head and so bespattered him about the eyes that he was glad to run off howling. Trim pursued him till he took refuge below; and then returned smiling to his master to receive his caresses.

During our circumnavigation of Australia in the years 1801, 2, and 3, Trim had frequent opportunities of repeating his observations and experiments in his favourite science, natural history, and of exerting his undiminished activity and zeal for the public good. In the Gulph of Carpentaria, from the unhealthiness of the climate, the want of his usual fresh food, and perhaps from too much application to study, this worthy creature became almost grey, lost much of weight, and seemed to be threatened with a premature old age; but to the great joy of his friends, he re-assumed his fine black robe and his accustomed portliness, a short time after returning to harbour.

Only once was Trim known to be guilty of theft: he had a soul above it; but one unlucky afternoon, a cold leg of mutton in the pantry tempted him. Being unable to carry it off himself, he got the assistance of Van, a Dutch cat on board; and they had so far succeeded as to get it down off the shelf, and were dragging it together into the hold; when lo! the steward came and surprised them in the fact. Van made his escape, but Trim, ever confident, made no efforts, and was seized and beaten soundly. He took the blows with philosophical patience; but no sooner was he set at liberty, than he ran after his false Dutch friend, and repaid him with interest the beating he had received. The recital of this unfortunate anecdote of my friend Trim, will I hope be received as a proof of the impartiality of this history; and I advertize the reader not to seek in it for any political allegory; but to be assured, that the facts were really such as they are here related.

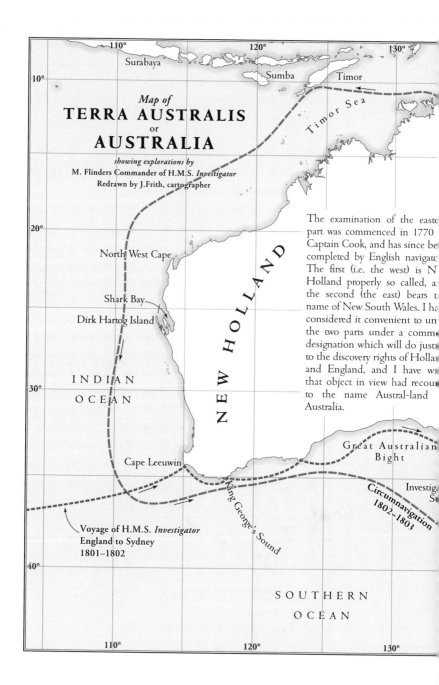

Map of
TERRA AUSTRALIS
or
AUSTRALIA

showing explorations by
M. Flinders Commander of H.M.S. *Investigator*
Redrawn by J.Frith, cartographer

Surabaya

Sumba

Timor

Timor Sea

110°

120°

130°

10°

20°

North West Cape

Shark Bay

Dirk Hartog Island

INDIAN

OCEAN

30°

NEW HOLLAND

The examination of the easte
part was commenced in 1770
Captain Cook, and has since be
completed by English navigato
The first (i.e. the west) is N
Holland properly so called, a
the second (the east) bears t
name of New South Wales. I ha
considered it convenient to un
the two parts under a comm
designation which will do just
to the discovery rights of Holla
and England, and I have w
that object in view had recou
to the name Austral-land
Australia.

Great Australian
Bight

Investig
S

Circumnavigation
1802–1803

Cape Leeuwin

King George's Sound

Voyage of H.M.S. *Investigator*
England to Sydney
1801–1802

40°

SOUTHERN

OCEAN

110°

120°

130°

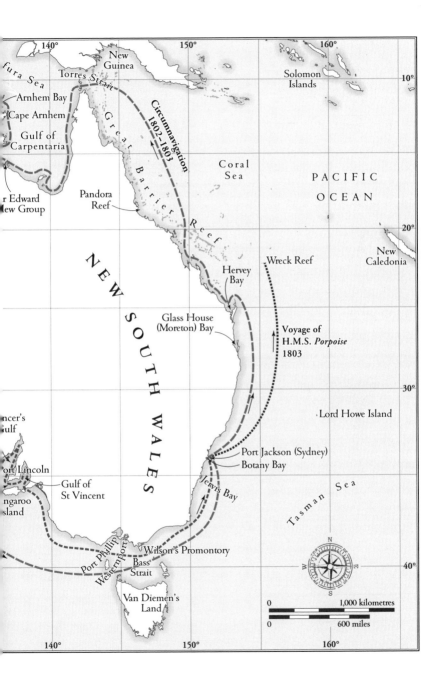

140° 150° 160°

fura Sea Torres Strait New Guinea Solomon Islands 10°

Arnhem Bay

Cape Arnhem

Gulf of Carpentaria Circumnavigation 1802–1803 Coral Sea PACIFIC OCEAN

r Edward ew Group Pandora Reef Great Barrier Reef 20°

NEW Wreck Reef New Caledonia

Hervey Bay

SOUTH Voyage of H.M.S. *Porpoise* 1803

Glass House (Moreton) Bay 30°

Lord Howe Island

ncer's ulf

WALES

ort Lincoln Gulf of St Vincent Port Jackson (Sydney) Botany Bay

ngaroo sland Jervis Bay Tasman Sea

Port Phillip Wilson's Promontory Westernport Bass Strait 40°

Van Diemen's Land

N W E S

0 1,000 kilometres

0 600 miles

The *Spyall* being found to be rotten,* Trim embarked on board His Majesty's ship the *Janty* to return to England, and was shipwrecked with us upon a coral bank in the Great Equinoxial Ocean† on the night of Aug. 17. 1803. The imagination can scarcely attain to what Trim had to suffer during this dreadful night, but his courage was not beat down. He got to Wreck-Reef Bank with the crew, and passed there two long and dreary months; during which his zeal in the provision tent was not less than it had been in the bread room, and his manners preserved all their amiability.

---

* *Investigator (Spyall)* leaked badly. After passing through Torres Strait, she was careened and the carpenters found so many rotten timbers they reckoned she'd founder in a gale, which forced Flinders to abandon the coastal survey. They made some running repairs in Timor and arrived back in Port Jackson on 9 June 1803 having completed the circumnavigation. Flinders and Trim sailed for Britain in HMS *Porpoise* (*Janty*) on 10 August 1803 to organise a replacement ship. They didn't get far. Seven days later they were shipwrecked on Wreck Reef. Taking command, Flinders and the captain of the *Cato*, with a 'double set of rowers', sailed the ship's cutter some 700 miles (1127 km) back to Port Jackson to organise rescue.

† 'The Great Equinoxial Ocean' is a term Flinders may well have borrowed from *A voyage round the world: performed during the years 1790, 1791, and 1792*, by Etienne Marchand, preceded by a historical introduction, and illustrated by charts, etc. Translated from the French of C.P. Claret Fleurieu (1801), it was possibly one of the many books on South Seas voyages in his cabin library.

Wreck of the Porpoise, William Westall. National Library of Australia.

When vessels arrived to our assistance, Trim preferred following his master on board the *Minikin* schooner, to going with the rest of the ship's company to China in a large vessel, giving thereby a memorable example of faithful attachment. The *Minikin* being very leaky, was obliged to stop at the Isle of France;* and there poor Trim, his master and few followers were all made prisoners; under the pretext that they had come to spy out the nakedness of the land; though it was clear as day, that they knew nothing of the war that had taken place a few months before. Trim was confined in a room with his master and another officer, and as he possessed more philosophy than we did, he contributed by his gay humour to soften our strait captivity; but sometimes also he contrived to elude the vigilance of the sentinel at the door, and left us to make little temporary excursions in the neighbourhood. It is probable that he made some new secret acquaintances in these visits, for they became more frequent than was prudent; and for fear of accidents, we were obliged to shut him up after supper.

---

* The small size of the *Cumberland* (referred to by Flinders as the *Minikin*) made it necessary to stop at every convenient place on the way to England for water and refreshment, explains Flinders in *In Terra Australis*. But back in 1803, news travelled very slowly. People on one side of the world had no idea what was happening on the other. That's why when Flinders dropped anchor in Port Louis on 17 December, he hadn't heard that Britain had declared war on France seven months earlier and that the Napoleonic Wars were on again. He was detained on Isle of France (Île de France), as Mauritius was then called, for the next six and a half years. The Dutch had established the colony of Mauritius (1638–1710), brought sugar cane and slavery there, and apparently wiped out the dodo. The French took over in 1710 and ruled until the British captured the island in 1810, the year Flinders finally made it home.

On our being removed to the Maison Despeaux amongst the prisoners of war, a French lady offered to be Trim's security, in order to have him for a companion to her little daughter; and the fear of some clandestine proceedings on the part of the soldiers of the guard, induced me to comply, on finding it would give no umbrage to His Excellency the French governor and captain general. A fortnight had scarcely passed, when the public gazette of the island announced that he was no where to be found; and offered a reward of ten Spanish dollars* – to any one who would

* For centuries, the Spanish dollar was the international currency.

conduct him back to his afflicted little mistress. My sorrow may be better conceived than described; I would with pleasure have given fifty dollars to have had my friend and companion restored to me. All research and offers of recompense were in vain, poor Trim was effectually lost; and it is but too probable, that this excellent unsuspecting animal was stewed and eaten by some hungry black slave, in whose eyes all his merits could not balance against the avidity excited by his sleek body and fine furred skin.

Thus perished my faithful intelligent Trim! The sporting, affectionate, and useful companion of my voyages during four years. Never, my Trim, "to take thee all in all, shall I see thy like again"; but never wilt thou cease to be regretted by all who had the pleasure of knowing thee. And for thy affectionate master and friend, – he promises thee, if ever he shall have the happiness to enjoy repose in his native country, under a thatched cottage surrounded by half an acre of land, to erect in the most retired corner, a monument to perpetuate thy memory and record thy uncommon merits; and this shall be thy epitaph.

To the memory of
Trim,
the best and most illustrious of his Race, -
the most affectionate of friends, –
faithful of servants,
and best of creatures.
He made the Tour of the Globe, and a voyage to
Australia,
which he circumnavigated; and was ever the
delight and pleasure of his fellow voyagers.
Returning to Europe in 1803, he was shipwrecked
in the Great Equinoxial Ocean;
This danger escaped, he sought refuge and assistance
at the Isle of France, where
he was made prisoner, contrary to the laws of
Justice, of Humanity, and of
French National Faith;
and where, alas! he terminated his useful
career, by an untimely death,
being devoured by the Catophagi*
of that island.
Many a time have I beheld his little merriments with delight,
and his superior intelligence with surprise:
Never will his like be seen again![†]
Trim was born in the Southern Indian Ocean, in the
year 1799, and
and [sic] perished as above at the Isle of France
in 1804.

Peace be to his shade, and
Honour to his memory

To the memory of

Trim,

the best and most illustrious of his Race,

the most affectionate of friends,

faithful of servants,

and best of creatures.

He made the Tour of the Globe, and a voyage to

Australia,

which he circumnavigated; and was ever the

delight and pleasure of his fellow voyagers.

Returning to Europe in 1803, he was shipwrecked

in the Great Equinoxial Ocean;

This danger escaped, he sought refuge and assistance

at the Isle of France, where

he was made prisoner, contrary to the laws of

Justice, of Humanity, and of

French National Faith;

and where, alas! he terminated his useful

career, by an untimely death,

being devoured by the Catophagi of

that island.

Many a time have I beheld his little merriments with delight,

and his superior intelligence with surprise:

Never will his like be seen again.

Trim was born in the Southern Indian Ocean, in the

Year 1799, and

and perished as above at the Isle of France

in 1804.

Peace be to his shade, and

Honour to his memory

---

* Flinders' wordplay: Anthropophagi are the 'man eaters' of literature from Herodotus onwards; here, Catophagi are the 'cat eaters'.

† 'Never, my Trim, to take thee all in all, shall I see thy like again' – a nod to Shakespeare: "Take him for all in all. I shall not look upon his like again," Hamlet, speaking of his father, says to Horatio.

Matthew Flinders: Trim's Shipmate and Bedfellow

Gillian Dooley
Researcher & Writer

Adelaide

On 11 January 1807 Matthew Flinders was at Plaines Wilhems on the island of Mauritius (then called Île de France) in the Indian Ocean, where he had already been detained by the French governor, General Charles-Mathieu-Isodore Decaen, for more than three years. Naturally he was very frustrated by that, but he kept himself busy. He wrote in his journal:

> When not otherwise occupied, I have lately employed myself, either in correcting my narrative, ... – in reading Grants history of the Isle of France and making notes upon it, – or in translating into French the history of my cat Trim, which I wrote out for the purpose.[1]

On the previous days he had been visiting his friend, the artist Toussaint Antoine de Chazal de Chamarel, who was painting his portrait.

The portrait M. Chazal was painting in December 1806 and January 1807 is now famous. It gives us the best idea we have of what Matthew looked like. Unsmiling, he fixes the viewer with a sombre, slightly stern gaze. His mouth is set in a determined line: he looks as if he hasn't had a shave for a day or two. Matthew described what M. Chazal was doing as 'tak[ing] a copy of my face, of the natural size'.[2]

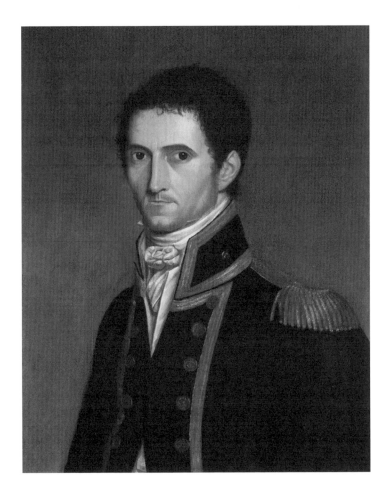

Portrait of Captain Matthew Flinders, RN, 1774–1814, Toussaint Antoine de Chazal de Chamarel. Art Gallery of South Australia.

It seems odd to us these days to sum up the creative process in this rather dismissive way – to describe painting a portrait as if it were merely 'taking a copy' of someone's face, and to use the term 'writing out' a story as if no art were involved in the telling of it. But, in the 18th and 19th centuries, it was common enough for writers to claim to be 'copying Nature'[3] or presenting 'a definite and substantial reality'.[4]

M. Chazal could have decided to paint Matthew as he was when he was laughing at one of his jokes, or arguing with him over a card game, or playing the flute to Mme Chazal's harpsichord accompaniment. But for him, the 'reality' of Matthew was to be captured with the use of measuring instruments. And for Matthew, the story of his cat Trim was just a matter of sitting down to write 'a history' that he could then use for French translation practice.

Was the 'history' he wrote in January 1807 *The Biographical Tribute to the Memory of Trim*? On the surviving manuscript he added 'Isle de France 1809' to the title. Maybe what he wrote in 1807 was a simpler version that he elaborated over the next two or three years. In any case, what we have is far from a simple 'history'.

There can't be many cats in history who have been described in such affectionate detail, and Trim now has his share of portraits and statues – so much so that it seems hardly proper nowadays to depict Matthew without his faithful Trim somewhere nearby. How lucky we are that somehow the manuscript of *Trim* survived among Matthew's papers, to be discovered in 1971 by Stephen Murray-Smith.[5] It has been published several times since then.

But outside this manuscript, what do we know about the real Trim? In all the 235,000 words of Flinders' private journal, he only mentioned him that one time, to say he was writing out his history. He didn't figure in the journal during the dark days when, according to the *Tribute*, 'confined in a room with his master and another officer, ... he contributed by his gay humour to soften our straight captivity'.

Matthew's letters give us a few more hints. He mentioned him twice in letters to his wife, Ann.

Ann would have known Trim from her short and ill-fated sojourn on board the *Investigator* between her marriage to Matthew on 17 April 1801 and the middle of June that year, when she was sent back to her family, banished from the voyage. Matthew wrote news of him from Sydney in June 1803 as one among several shipmates: 'Trim, like his master is becoming grey; he is at present fat and frisky, and takes meat from ones forks with his former dexterity: he is commonly my bedfellow.'[6]

In November 1804, he wrote to Ann again, this time from the Garden Prison in Mauritius. At the end of a long, passionate letter, he added a teasing paragraph directed towards 'that idle thing, Belle' – Ann's teenage half-sister Isabella Tyler. 'Does she think I will bring her any pretty feathers or little fishes when she has not written me one line for these live-long three years last past?' He catalogued a whole lot of presents that Isabella wouldn't get, and one of them was 'a set of Trim's finger nails which he shed in the Gulph of Carpentaria.'[7]

Trim gets a mention in one more letter. This one was to Governor Philip Gidley King, written in September 1803 at sea in the tiny schooner *Cumberland*, which Matthew had decided to sail all the way to England even though nobody had ever been so far in such a small vessel. Of course he didn't make it – he stopped at the French colony of Île de France (Mauritius) to repair the ship, and he, Trim and the rest of the dozen crew were taken prisoner by the French.

But when he wrote to Governor King he didn't know what awaited him and he was in a jovial mood. He wrote, 'of all the filthy little things I ever saw, this schooner, for bugs, lice, fleas, weavels, mosquitos, cockroaches large and small, and mice, rises superior to them all'. He described the measures they were taking against the various insects, with the bugs being the most persistent: he suggested that 'before this vile bug-like smell will leave me, [I] must, I believe, as well as my clothes, undergo a good boiling in the large kettle'.

The rodents, however, were easily dealt with: 'I shall set my old friend Trim to work upon the mice.'[8] He knew he could rely on his 'faithful, intelligent ... sporting, affectionate and useful' feline friend.

Through all his trials and tribulations, Matthew was always dreaming about retiring to the English countryside to live quietly with Ann. And, 'if ever he shall have the happiness to enjoy repose in his native country', there would be a place for Trim: 'under a thatched cottage surrounded by half an acre of land ... in the most retired corner, a monument to perpetuate thy memory and record thy uncommon merits'.

Sadly, that never happened. But Trim's memory has now been restored and perpetuated to the point that he is now one of history's most famous cats. His affectionate master and friend did him proud. At the same time, as Stephen Murray-Smith writes, *Trim* 'tells us as much about [Matthew's] personality and humanity as, perhaps, the rest of his published work does in total'.[9] In writing this loving, witty, moving tribute to Trim, Matthew Flinders revealed a side of himself that we wouldn't otherwise suspect had ever existed.

Incidentally ...

There are now memorials to Flinders and Trim in Australia, Britain and Mauritius. Not many ships' cats have one memorial, let alone six. The first one, by John Cornwell, was erected in 1996 on a window sill of the State Library of New South Wales, behind the 1925 statue of Matthew. Trim was included in a Flinders memorial plaque erected in Baie du Cap on Mauritius, near where Matthew lived for nearly five years while he was detained on the island. There is a statue of Matthew in the town square of his home town of Donington, Lincolnshire, with Trim winding around his left leg. It was erected in 2006.

The most recent major statue of Trim and Matthew is in the concourse outside Euston Station in London, not far from St James's Churchyard, where Matthew was buried. It was designed and created by Mark Richards for an international committee determined to erect a permanent memorial in the city where Matthew spent his last few years. Prince William unveiled the statue on the bicentenary of his death, 19 July 2014.

In 1911, George Gordon McCrae described his ideal for a statue of Matthew:

> The figure, of course, of heroic size, and in a working undress of the period, the pose easy and natural, the feet planted on a coralline rock, with a few sea shells and weed, and perhaps a star-fish 'en evidence' – his quadrant laid against the inner surface of his flexed left arm, while he reads off the bearing from the vernier of the instrument, the fingers of the right hand grasping the pencil, with which he is about to record it.[10]

Matthew Flinders, Capt. R.N. 1809, author of Trim, *George Gordon McCrae. National Library of Australia.*

McCrae's notion for a statue of a working chartmaker rather than a uniformed hero had to wait for nearly a century to be realised – and Mark Richards went one better, by adding Trim sitting patiently behind Flinders while he works. According to the Matthew Flinders Memorial Statue website, 'Richards was struck not so much by his representing the grand ambitions of king and country as by the day-to-day reality of his seafaring life; the discipline, organisation, unimaginable privations and determination... With all this in mind, Mark Richards presents Matthew not as a distant heroic figure, but as a man among us.'[11]

Whenever I'm in London, I visit Matthew and Trim at Euston, and I enjoy watching children stroking and patting Trim while their parents drink coffee at the surrounding café tables.

Full-sized copies of Mark Richards' statue of Flinders and Trim have now been installed at Flinders University and in Port Lincoln, both in South Australia. There are also dozens of miniature versions (maquettes) around the world, bought by Flinders' enthusiasts, local councils, educational institutions and historical societies. When Barack and Michelle Obama visited the Duke and Duchess of Cambridge in London in June 2015, the publicity photo shows Trim and Matthew just over Michelle's shoulder.

My Seafurring Adventures with Matt Flinders

TRIM

Isle of France

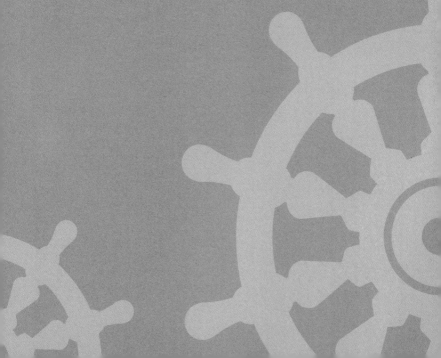

Preface

There was never a dull moment with Matt, first on the *Reliance*, then on the *Norfolk* to Moreton Bay and then on the *Investigator*, lapping and mapping Australia's coastline. As if that wasn't enough for a CV, we were then shipwrecked in the *Porpoise* on Wreck Reef when Matt was hurrying home with all his charts and journals, and finally we were taken prisoner on Mauritius when we simply stopped by in the *Cumberland* for essential repairs and provisions. How were we to know a war was on?

It's nice to have had someone write a Biographical Tribute to me, but the announcement of my death was rather premature. Matt should have had more faith in my true grit and survival skills. That's why I thought it important to set the record straight (for posterity) by rounding out the stories he tells in the *Tribute*, filling in the gaps, and making the odd correction or three.

It seemed to me that an 'incidental memoir' approach using snippets from the *Tribute* as a springboard for my tale would be the best way to share my story (and marry it with Matt's version of events). I roped in the services of a couple of scribes to help me pull all this together, but the opinions are entirely mine, and I have clearly signposted them as 'according to Trim' so there's no misunderstanding.

Trim

Incident 1

*'This good-natured purring animal was born on board His Majesty's ship the **Roundabout** in 1799 during a passage from the Cape of Good Hope to Botany Bay.'*

ACCORDING TO TRIM

The '1799' is either a slip of the pen or a slip of the memory. I was born two years earlier in 1797 on the *Reliance* (called the *Roundabout* by Matt). By 1799, Matt was in command of the *Norfolk*, completing the circumnavigation of Van Diemen's Land with George Bass, then heading north with me and Bongaree (our indispensable guide on all local matters) to Glass-House Bay and Hervey's Bay on the lookout for a large river system so he could explore the interior. Spoiler alert: no luck there.

My parents had signed on as ships' cats on the *Reliance* under the command of Henry Waterhouse for the 1795 Botany Bay trip, taking Captain John Hunter out to his new job as second governor of the fledgling penal colony. Bennelong was also on board, heading home after three years in England, and the crew included the dynamite Lincolnshire duo George Bass (surgeon) and Matthew Flinders (master's mate). Waterhouse had already been to Botany Bay – he was a First Fleeter (a midshipman on the

Sirius). So he knew where he was going. And had some idea what it was like out there.

They left Plymouth on 15 February, arrived in Sydney seven months later and, after repairs to leaky planks and a round trip to Norfolk Island, set sail for Cape Town in September 1796 – Waterhouse had a commission to buy livestock for the colony there. He certainly stocked up, stowing 109 head of cattle, 107 sheep and three mares on board plus fodder. He wasn't exaggerating when he claimed: 'I believe no ship ever went to sea so much lumbered.' While a typical navy supply ship might carry 60 or 70 head of cattle, the *Reliance* was carrying nearly four times that.

Thus 'lumbered', they left Cape Town in April 1797 bound for Botany Bay, and somewhere in the middle of the Indian Ocean I arrived on the scene, hence Matt's throwaway line about my roots, 'Indian by birth'.

Incidentally ...

The Cape Town trip was the game changer for the colony. Twenty-six of the sheep stowed on board were 'Spanish sheep' (merinos) renowned for producing the finest wool in the world, and Waterhouse owned them – he had snapped them up at four pounds a head after others had knocked them back. That was the easy bit. Getting them back to Botany Bay was the hard bit. It was an appalling trip at times, with 'the sea breaking over the ship with shocks that are inconceivable, a few more of which I am well convinc'd must have sent her to the bottom,' says Waterhouse.[12] They also ran out of fodder for the livestock, so 'we fed them – or rather forc'd them – to eat the seamen's biscuit, & any other messes we could make up'. Despite this, he landed 24 of his 26 merinos, kept some to breed on his Parramatta River property, and sold the rest to John Macarthur (who had offered 15 guineas a head for the lot), Samuel Marsden and Captain Rowley. Within forty years, the colony was 'riding on the sheep's back', producing more than two million kilos (4.4 million pounds) of wool a year.

Riding the sheep's back ...

Hey!

How did the King of Spain's 'not-for-export' prize merinos get to the Cape in the first place? In 1789, the Spanish king gave William of Orange some sheep from his Escoriale Merino Stud, and William, in turn, 'gave', as an experiment, a couple of rams and four ewes to Colonel Jacob Gordon, military commander at the Cape, to see if they would fare better there than they had done in the wet, cold Netherlands. Gordon, who probably couldn't believe his luck when six prize merinos arrived, sent them off to breed on the Dutch East India Company farm, Groenekloof. But he didn't live to build himself a wool empire in South Africa; he committed suicide in 1795 after copping substantial abuse for surrendering the Cape to the invading British. His widow gave six merinos away, sold the rest to Waterhouse, and left the Cape for good.

BACKGROUND BRIEFING:
Bound for Botany Bay

The American War of Independence had put an end to Britain's efficient and effective system of sending its felons elsewhere since the 1717 Transportation Act. Everywhere they had tried to send them since had said no thanks very firmly, including the local authorities in Belize (British Honduras), Jamaica, Newfoundland and Nova Scotia, Cape Coast Castle (Ghana), and Tristan da Cunha. And when the dust had settled after the American War of Independence, the Maryland Government turned them down flat. The felons of course kept coming, the gaols were full to overflowing and the hulks – the temporary prisons on unseaworthy ships moored offshore – were massively overcrowded. It was a problem. Then Botany Bay was 'discovered'. Now that would be the perfect place for a penal colony, reckoned the British Government.

Someone did some sums that showed transporting convicts to Botany Bay would be cheaper than building more jails at home. Others noted the bonus: returning would be difficult, so they'd more than likely be gone for good. Best of all, unlike everywhere else that had turned them down, Botany Bay was open for business. There was no one there to say no. It was terra nullius, they said, ignoring the fact it was actually already inhabited. So that's why Captain Arthur Phillip's First Fleet was bound for Botany Bay in 1787. He dropped anchor on 19 January 1788, had a look around, gave the thumbs-down and sailed north round the next headland, proclaiming the new colony of New South Wales on 26 January from the landing site at Port Jackson in what he called Sydney Cove (after the man who drafted his instructions). But people had in their heads that Botany Bay was going to be the name of the new penal colony, so it stuck.

Stepping ashore on Port Jackson, Phillip probably raised the flag with some relief. But it wasn't the first time the English colours had fluttered over Terra Australis. Captain James Cook had hoisted the flag on Possession Island on 22 August 1770 when, following Admiralty orders, he took possession of the eastern coast of New Holland in the name of His Majesty King George the Third. In his heart of hearts, he probably couldn't see the point as he noted in his Journal that the country produced nothing that 'can become an Article in trade to invite Europeans to fix settlement upon it.' But it wasn't trade they needed in 1788. It was a dumping ground for convicts.

Captain Cook taking possession of the Australian Continent on behalf of the British Crown, 1770, under the name of New South Wales. Samuel Calvert. National Library of Australia.

Incident 2

'In playing with his little brothers and sisters upon deck by moon-light, when the ship was lying tranquilly in harbour, the energy and elasticity of his movements sometimes carried him so far beyond his mark, that he fell overboard; but this was far from being a misfortune; he learned to swim and to have no dread of the water.'

ACCORDING TO TRIM

The harbour that the *Reliance* was lying tranquilly in was Port Jackson, where she was undergoing repairs after that rough voyage from Cape Town. Captain Cook had spotted its entrance when sailing past on 6 May 1770 and named it. He reckoned it looked like a good anchorage. 'Spot on!' said First Fleet Captain Arthur Phillip, who, on 15 May 1788, proclaimed it 'the finest harbour in the world, in which a thousand sail of the line may ride in the most perfect security' and a far better option than sandy, swampy Botany Bay that was lacking in fresh water and way too shallow for ships.

And that's where I 'learned' to swim. Though of course I didn't 'learn' to swim. I already could swim. I was doing what comes naturally to most land animals, who can swim if they have to/want to; people and apes are the notable exceptions. *They* have to learn.

Felines have a natural buoyancy, so all we have to do when we hit water by design or accident is keep our nose above the waves, keep breathing, keep paddling and keep calm (or as calm as possible in big seas). Unlike the dogs on board, however, we generally don't choose to swim, because getting wet is a problem for us. Fur takes hours to lick dry once water soaks through both the top coat and the undercoat. Turkish van cats, known as 'swimming cats', are different. They don't mind getting wet because they don't have an undercoat like regular cats and their top coat is virtually moisture resistant.

Incidentally ...

Naming things is what navigators do so they can put them on their maps and others can find them and know where they are. First on the scene gets naming rights. Few European explorers were the first on the scene, but they were the first explorers with compasses, chronometers, sextants and charts, enabling them to map places and give them names. Captain James Cook named more than a hundred bays, capes and notable features as he sailed up the east coast of New Holland. Botany Bay he named after 'the great quantity of new plants collected by Mr Banks and Dr Solander' [they were the naturalists on board *Endeavour*]',[13]

View of Port Jackson taken from the South Head, William Westall;
engraved by John Pye. National Library of Australia.

striking out the earlier contenders Sting Ray Harbour, Botanist Harbour and Botanist Bay. Port Jackson was personal: a nod to his friend and admiralty secretary George Jackson, a man who later changed his name to Duckett to meet the provisions of a will. Port Jackson, however, remained Port Jackson.

Of course, that's not what the locals called it. The traditional Eora people had plenty of names for their places, but few newcomers or passers-by bothered to ask what they were. William Dawes was an exception. His First Fleet job was to make astronomical observations during the voyage to Botany Bay and then set up an observatory to monitor a comet expected in the southern hemisphere in 1788. He built the observatory, but the comet didn't show. He then worked as an engineer and surveyor. But his lasting claim to fame is what he did in his spare time: he recorded the local languages in numerous notebooks because he thought it was important. He wanted to stick around the young colony and do more, but he made himself unpopular with Governor Phillip by opposing a punitive expedition against a group of Aborigines in December 1790, and as payback, Phillip dispatched him back to Britain when his time was up in December 1791. He took his notebooks with him.

As for Matthew Flinders, he named about 348 Australian places during his four voyages, and most of them are still gazetteered and in use today. However, he really only made suggestions for names rather than plonking them down immediately on his charts. As he writes in a memoir in 1805:

> 66 Very few names are applied by me; for where I could not find a descriptive one, it was left to the Admiralty, or those whom their Lordships might chuse, to apply a name. It is not only consistent with propriety that the planners and promoters of a voyage of discovery should have a principle share in affixing names to the discovered parts, but it is necessary that the baptizing mania of some navigators should be under control, to prevent so many repetitions of names as we find in different parts of the world; nay sometimes in the same part. If such a controuling power had been vested in the hydrographer of the Admiralty, we should not have had two Cape Howes upon the south coast of Australia, or two Cape Deliverances upon the south coast of New Guinea.[14] 99

Incident 3

'His exercises commenced with acquiring the art of leaping over the hands; and as every man in the ship took pleasure in instructing him, he at length arrived to such a pitch of perfection, that I am persuaded, had nature placed him in the empire of Lilliput, his merit would have promoted him to the first offices in the state.'

ACCORDING TO TRIM

Sailors do get time off. Matt thought this important. He organised dancing to the fife and drum on the forecastle on fine evenings and, as he puts it, 'did not discourage other playful amusements which might occasionally be more to the taste of the sailors'.[15] One of those was teaching me tricks. And as I have never minded being the centre of attention, a good time was had by all, with tasty little rewards on occasion.

Activities like leaping over hands or chasing a musket ball on a piece of twine or along the deck also provided opportunities to exercise and to practise the stalking, pouncing and leaping skills that are essential for rodent control. So what looks like play is actually work, and a pleasant way to socialise with shipmates and to stay on top of one's game.

Doing my bit keeping the rats and mice down and out was one of my duties, and it's true, as Matt remarks in the *Tribute*, that I was known for dashing after prey through thick and thin like a man of war. He knew he could always rely on my zeal in the hold and bread room to protect the ship's stores. He had ordered 30,000 pounds of biscuit, 8,000 pounds of flour and 156 bushels of kiln-dried wheat, plus Indian corn as fodder for the sheep, pigs, geese and fowl, for the long voyage ahead circumnavigating Australia in the *Investigator*. I had to be indefatigable. Rats and mice would take one look and think this was an invitation to dine at a never-ending banquet.

I'm not going to claim any ratting records, but I like to think I brought to rodent control the same determined and methodical approach Matt brought to navigation and charting. I was very touched by his commendation in the *Tribute* that I 'possessed a degree of patience and perseverance, of which few men can boast; and ... that like a faithful subject, ... employed all these estimable qualities in the service of His Majesty's faithful servants, and indirectly of His Majesty himself'.

Incidentally ...

Successful hunting is not hit and miss. The ratting record holders enhance their hit rate with these seven highly effective habits – although they are listed here in some sort of ranking order, all of them are important:

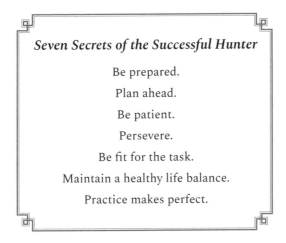

Seven Secrets of the Successful Hunter

Be prepared.

Plan ahead.

Be patient.

Persevere.

Be fit for the task.

Maintain a healthy life balance.

Practice makes perfect.

Incident 4

'Trim took a fancy to learning nautical astronomy. When an officer took lunar or other observations, he would place himself by the time-keeper, and consider the motion of the hands, and apparently the uses of the instrument, with much earnest attention.'

ACCORDING TO TRIM

Like all felines, my navigation is very good on terra firma. I can find my way round a new neighbourhood easily, which is what I did when holed up in Mauritius. I would have gone stir crazy if I hadn't been able to stretch my legs now and then. So, I slipped past the sentry and checked out the lie of the land. I never had any problems finding my way 'home', if our prison could be called that. Felines have a good sense of direction, but for navigational aids it's mostly down to our sense of smell. The nose knows, you could say. At sea, we are all at sea. Dogs are in the same boat.

Humans are different. They use their eyes rather than their nose and over the years have come up with a swag of navigational aids (compass, sextant, time-keeper or chronometer) to make their nautical-astronomy observations more accurate. Matt was very methodical about this. When he was charting a coastline, he took each bearing and angle himself from either the deck or the masthead, and then overnight he'd plot the results. Next morning, he was back at it, starting from the spot where he'd ended the previous day's work.

Taking the bearings is one of those tasks that put structure into a day's work, which is why I liked to keep him and the time-keeper company. There's a sense of doing important work when you're charting a coastline that hasn't been charted before. I'm not surprised he became renowned as one of the world's most accomplished navigators. His charts show his meticulous attention to detail as well as, returning the compliment, his patience, perseverance and, dare I say it, earnest attention.

Incidentally ...

Matt made a major contribution to navigation with his practical investigations into the influence of magnetism on the compass needle. When we were surveying Australia's south coast, he noticed that when the ship's heading changed, there was a perplexing difference in the direction of the magnetic needle that he couldn't account for. He had a theory that iron might be part of the problem and moved a couple of cannons. But it wasn't as simple as that. Stuck in a room on Mauritius with time on his hands, he gave the problem more thought, and wrote a paper setting out his findings – *Concerning the Differences in the Magnetic Needle, on Board the* Investigator, *Arising from an Alteration in the Direction of the Ship's Head* – and prudently called for more research to be carried out.

While he was occupying himself with his charts and notes, I imprudently occupied myself exploring Port Louis, testing my personal navigation system. It never failed me.

Incident 5

'He knew what good discipline required, and on taking in a reef, never presumed to go aloft until the order was issued; but so soon as the officer had given the word – "Away up aloft!" Up he jumped along with the seamen; and so active and zealous was he, that none could reach the top before, or so soon as he did.'

ACCORDING TO TRIM

No surprises that practical seamanship had a greater appeal than nautical astronomy. Likewise, I was very happy doing my pest control stint in the bread room and in the holds, but the real attraction was going aloft. Sitting up there on the cap I could keep an eye on the whole ship, my home range. I freely admit that my role was principally supervisory – the topmen did the hard work taking a reef in the sails (shortening the sail by reducing the area exposed to the wind) or replacing a topmast that had been carried away. These topmen were the absolute elite, chosen to work high above the deck on the masts and yards. It was not a job for everyone. Many sailors hate heights.

Saying none could reach the top before me is exaggerating. But racing to the top was a breeze for me because we cats are natural climbers with built-in crampon claws. Coming down was another story, and I'm not sure what evolution's plan was here. Our claws are simply not designed for ease of descent – it's very hard to get a grip because they point the wrong way. Of course, we can climb down if we have to, but going head first can be very unwise, and backing down is not a good look in anyone's book and not a smart move with predators around. Having the sense to put ego aside and hitch a ride with a mate is a good call. Mateship is what it's all about on board – providing your shipmates with support and companionship in times of need. Worst-case scenario? Jumping. It isn't always a nine-lives extreme challenge. Cats are designed

to make a perfect landing on all four paws. Mostly. This is because within 0.125 to 0.5 of a second, a falling cat can safely turn over in its own standing height. In fact, it's been described as a gold-medal performance, achieving a net rotation while keeping total angular momentum constant and sticking the perfect landing. Of course, having a flexible backbone and no functional collarbone (clavicle) helps with aerial acrobatics. As in all things, practice makes perfect, and experience is a great teacher. The righting reflex (also called air righting) begins to appear in kittens at three to four weeks of age, and they have perfected it by six to seven weeks.

Incidentally ...

Few animals (and *Homo sapiens* isn't among them) can climb down head first. Controlling descent (that is, opposing the force of gravity, which is pulling you down) is the problem. Those that can head down head first have highly mobile ankle joints and claws. That list is short: there are a couple of felines (the margay and the clouded leopard), red pandas, the slender mongoose, the fossa (a cat-like relative of the mongoose), and racoons and squirrels, who can rotate their feet 180 degrees. That's like having reversible feet or paws. No mean feat.

Incident 6

'In an expedition made to examine the northern parts of the coast of New South Wales, Trim presented a request to be of the party, promising to take upon himself the defence of our bread bags, and his services were accepted.'

ACCORDING TO TRIM

The key role of ships' cats, or seafurrers, as they like to be called, was pest control, and I was renowned for my expertise in discharging my duties in this respect. Hence my vigilance in the bread room, the favourite haunt of mice and rats, and my undivided attention to the bread bags on the *Norfolk*, each of which had about a hundredweight of ship's biscuit. This is a major responsibility because bread is staple fare – a seaman gets a pound (about half a kilo) of it a day to give him the get-up-and-go he needs to sail the ship.

The bread in those bags faced a double whammy: attack from both within and without. There's not much we ships' cats can do about attack from within: the weevils are already hard at work in the bread that's in the bags. Attack from without is a different matter. We happily deal with the rodents, providing a complete catch-and-clean-up service.

While I occasionally enjoyed a little bread well dunked in milk on the *Reliance* thanks to William the gunroom steward, it isn't a natural part of the feline diet and not something I crave. We are meat eaters, or 'obligate carnivores', to use the technical term. Bongaree appreciated this and generously shared remnants of black swan from his kid with me. We were well supplied with swan on this trip as Flinders bagged 18 birds in Moreton Bay. Fresh is best as they say, and swan is a lot better than salt beef.

Bongaree and I had sailed together before when he had signed on for a 60-day Norfolk Island round trip on *Reliance* between May and July 1798, but this trip on the *Norfolk* was the first occasion we had time to get to know each other. He was the first Aboriginal I met; I was possibly the first ship's cat he met. We bonded. While the Eora people did keep pets such as dingo puppies, they had never had cats or kittens because there weren't any. We don't know when the first felines set foot on Terra Australis; but when Sydney Cove was being settled, a number of ships' cats jumped ship on arrival and called Australia home. Doing that never occurred to me. Seafaring with Matt suited me fine.

Incidentally ...

The *Norfolk*, a 25-ton sloop built on Norfolk Island using Norfolk Island pine, was originally intended to ship supplies and dispatches between Sydney and that penal colony on a more regular basis. She completed her first run to Port Jackson on 15 June 1798, and that decided it. She had a greater destiny. Governor Hunter immediately commandeered her for Flinders and Bass to circumnavigate Van Diemen's Land and prove that it was an island. They did. Flinders then sailed north in her to explore Glass-house Bay and Hervey's Bay, and Trim joined him for this trip.

That was not the end of the *Norfolk*'s adventures. In November 1800, laden with 500 bushels of wheat, she was seized by 15 convicts who had boarded her in Broken Bay on her way to Port Jackson from the Hawkesbury River.

> **"** The runaways proposed proceeding to the Dutch settlements among the Moluccas ... [and] called in at the Hunter River, where their vessel was driven on shore ... With all speed Governor King despatched an armed boat to the Hunter River, where the *Norfolk* was found bilged through the unskilful handling of the pirates, who thereupon committed a fresh act of piracy by seizing another boat. The armed cutter, after a desperate chase, captured nine out of the fifteen desperadoes, and secured the Sydney trader's vessel uninjured, but the *Norfolk* went to pieces in the surf off the point afterwards denominated Pirates' Point, and now known as Stockton.[16] **"**

BACKGROUND BRIEFING:
Baking Biscuit

Baking biscuit for Britain's navy was big business. Here's how big:

> At Deptford the bake-house belonging to the victualling-office has twelve ovens; each of which bakes twenty shoots daily; the quantity of flour used for each shoot is two bushels, or 112 pounds; which baked, produce 102 pounds of biscuit. Ten pounds are regularly allowed on each shoot for shrinkage, &c. ... at Deptford alone, they can furnish bread, daily, for 24,480 men, independent of Portsmouth and Plymouth..[17]

Incident 7

'In 1800, the Roundabout returned to England by the way of Cape Horn and St. Helena, and thus Trim, besides his other voyages, completed the tour of the globe.'

Well, this goes down in history as one of our rare uneventful voyages with nothing to do except observe 'small quadrupeds, birds, and flying fish'. However, without being picky, I have to insert a small correction: I hadn't yet completed a tour of the globe. That date with destiny had to wait until I completed the Portsmouth–Cape Town leg on the *Investigator*.

All told, we spent nearly a year in England, twelve long months when I discovered that the restrictions of hearth and home weren't for me (and I tried several that year). While I was being billeted around and trying to make friends with the locals, Matt was busy. He published his charts of his new discoveries (printed by John Nichols in London in 1801 and wisely dedicated to Sir Joseph Banks, the work was called *Observations on the Coasts of Van Diemen's Land, on Bass's Strait and Its Islands, and on Part of the Coasts of New South Wales: intended to accompany the charts of the*

late discoveries in those countries), and took time out to marry his sweetheart, Ann Chappelle. However, he didn't have long-term plans to settle down either. He had more explorations in mind.

He successfully pitched his plan to complete the investigation of the coasts of Terra Australis to the powers that be, and took command of the *Investigator* on a salary of £250 a year, which seemed princely but was somewhat less than the artists on board, he later discovered. Sir Joseph Banks' support magically opened doors for him. I didn't get to meet the great man myself, but people were always talking about him and his scientific achievements, and I personally noted his generosity and thoughtfulness – he presented Matt with a complete set of *Encyclopedia Britannica* for the use of all the officers on the voyage. I am pretty sure he also provided a signed copy of his own book, *Rules for Collecting and Preserving Specimens of Plants.*

Incidentally ...

Banks was always in the wings pulling strings. He had joined James Cook's scientific expedition to the Pacific in 1768 on the recommendation of the Royal Society. Cook's scientific mission was to calculate the distance between the earth and the sun by measuring Venus transiting the sun. Banks had his own plans. He was young, ambitious and wealthy and he wanted to be the first naturalist to go plant hunting and species seeking in the South Seas. And he was (as far as we know). Three years later, he and the Swedish naturalist Daniel Solander arrived back in England with some 30,000 plants, shells, insects and animals representing some 3,000 species, of which 1,600 were wholly new to science. He was also on the spot when Cook hoisted English colours and took possession of the whole eastern coast of New Holland in the name of His Majesty King George III on 22 August 1770, naming this new 'colony' New South Wales.

Sailing away, Cook came to the gloomy conclusion that 'the Country itself, so far as we know, doth not produce any one thing that can become an Article in Trade to invite Europeans to fix a settlement upon it'.[18] Banks was more of an optimist. He had a keen interest in New Holland from this time until his death, and repeatedly promoted the benefits of Botany Bay as a penal colony after the loss of the American colonies.

Incident 8

'During our circumnavigation of Australia in the years 1801, 2, and 3, Trim had frequent opportunities of repeating his observations and experiments in his favourite science, natural history, and of exerting his undiminished activity and zeal for the public good.'

In January 1801, Matt was appointed captain of the *Investigator* – 'a north-country-built ship, of three-hundred and thirty-four tons; and, in form, nearly resembl[ing] the description of vessel recommended by Captain Cook as best calculated for voyages of discovery', is how he described her. Six months later, the Admiralty gave us our sailing instructions to explore in detail, among other places, that part of the south Australian coastline then referred to as 'the Unknown Coast', and to document its flora and fauna. First stop Madeira, then Cape Town, and finally we dropped anchor in the sheltered waters of King George's Sound on 8 December. It had been a long haul of some four and a half months, but on the last leg we averaged over six knots on some days (or around 160 nautical miles a day).

During the circumnavigation, I generally stayed on board the *Investigator,* keeping an eye on things, when Matt and the botanical gentlemen led by Mr Brown went ashore to do their scientific work. Botanical work involves a lot of bodies, I discovered. Most of the quadrupeds and birds brought on board were dead on arrival because it's not easy to draw animals that won't sit still. A large speckled yellow snake was a rare living specimen. Matt and Mr Thistle captured it rather ingeniously: Matt pressed the butt end of his musket on the snake's neck while Mr Thistle sewed up

Thistle Island, a snake, William Westall. National Library of Australia.

its mouth with needle and twine. Mr Bauer (who often stayed on board too) didn't draw it, but Mr Westall did.

As Matt remarks, I certainly had frequent opportunities to add to my observations and experiments in natural history, most of them watching Mr Bauer industriously draw his preserved specimens on little pieces of paper. I don't think I was alone in finding the quadrupeds and birds more interesting than the plants, but Mr Brown was keen to have plants, so plants it mostly was. As for Mr Bauer's industriousness, he had sketched over 1,000 plants and 200 animals by the time we tacked between the heads of Port Jackson and dropped anchor in Sydney Cove at the end of the circumnavigation on 9 June 1803. That's a lot of sharp pencils. And many small sheets of paper that measured just 4½ inches by 6½ inches (11.5 cm x 16.5 cm) that he crowded with drawings because he didn't want to run out of paper. The humid weather tended to ruin paper with nasty mouldy stains.

Incident 9

'Trim embarked on board His Majesty's ship the **Janty** *to return to England, and was shipwrecked with us upon a coral bank in the Great Equinoxial Ocean on the night of Aug. 17. 1803... He got to Wreck-Reef Bank with the crew, and passed there two long and dreary months; during which his zeal in the provision tent was not less than it had been in the bread room, and his manners preserved all their amiability.'*

ACCORDING TO TRIM

When Matt sailed back to Port Jackson in the ship's cutter to arrange for our rescue, I stayed behind on the sand bank with the 94 other survivors and the sheep, who had unhelpfully trampled over some of William Westall's drawings when they were being driven ashore.

Mindful of the old saying that rats abandon a sinking ship, I maintained a constant watch on the provisions tent, which was packed with supplies that had to last us on full allowance until we were rescued.

There was more natural history to observe and examine on this sandy cay than in many parts of the continent we had just circumnavigated. Mr Brown and Mr Bauer would have enjoyed botanising here, but they had stayed behind in Sydney. Mr Bauer would have had to draw his pictures very quickly though, as the specimens went straight into the cooking pot. We enjoyed a remarkably varied diet for the six weeks we were stuck here, including birds, fish, shellfish, turtle and eggs (bird and turtle). Of course, there were some culinary disasters. No one asked for seconds the night cook served up sea cucumbers in his improvised version of trepang soup.

Everyone was pleased to see Matt back with the rescue ships and welcomed him with three very hearty cheers and an eleven-gun salute. Within days we were packed up and ready to roll. Some of the men returned to Port Jackson in the *Francis* to sign off; most boarded the *Rolla* for China, and ten joined us on the *Cumberland* heading straight for England as time was of the essence.

We left the reef with one mystery unsolved: who had been here before us? The *Porpoise* and the *Cato* weren't the first ships to be wrecked on the reef, for on our first night, the men had built a roaring fire with a worm-eaten and almost rotten spar and a piece of timber which, reckoned the master of the *Porpoise*, was part of the stern-post of a ship of about 400 tons. Matt thought they might have been from La Perouse's ships, which had set sail from Sydney in 1788 never to be seen again.

View of Wreck Reef bank taken at low water, Terra Australis,
William Westall. National Library of Australia.

The tents you can see in the illustration were improvised from
sails and spars recovered from the wreck. Young William Westall's
paintings of the shipwreck provide an important record of events.
Two years before, in 1801, he'd been appointed landscape artist for
the *Investigator* expedition at a salary of 300 guineas per year and
made a large number of pencil-and-wash landscapes and a series
of coast profiles in pencil to be included in the official record
of the circumnavigation. While many were 'wetted and partly
destroyed' when the *Porpoise* ran aground, a considerable number

were restored when he finally reached Britain in the *Rolla*. One of the originals still bears the hoof marks sheep made when young John Franklin (yes, the same John Franklin who later became governor of Tasmania and who was lost seeking the Northwest Passage) was driving them on to the reef and they accidentally trampled over some of the drawings.

BACKGROUND BRIEFING:
Wreck to Rescue

On 8 September 1803, sunburnt, salt-caked and unshaven, Flinders and his shipmates staggered ashore in Sydney Cove, much to the surprise of Governor King, who was at dinner with his family. The *Sydney Gazette* and the *New South Wales Advertiser* published the following accounts of the wreck, including Matthew Flinders' letter to Governor King, on Sunday 11 September and Sunday 18 September:

POSTSCRIPT

CAPTAIN FLINDERS, late Commander of His Majesty's Sloop Investigator, and Mr. PARK, Commander of the Ship Cato, arrived at Government House at half past 3 in the Afternoon of the 8th Instant, with the following disgreeable Intelligence, as communicated in the following LETTER to His EXCELLENCY.

Sydney, New South Wales,

Sept. 9, 1803.

SIR,

I have to inform you of my arrival here yesterday, in a Six-oar'd Cutter belonging to His Majesty's Armed Vessel PORPOISE, commanded by Lieut. FOWLER; which Ship, I am sorry to state to Your Excellency, I left on shore upon a Coral Reef, without any prospect of her being saved, in Latitude 22° 11' South, and Longitude 155° 13' East, being 196 miles to the N. 38° E. from Sandy Cape, and 729 miles from this Port: The Ship CATO, which was in Company, is entirely lost upon the same Reef, and broken to pieces without any thing having been saved from her; but the crew, with the exception of Three, are with the Whole of the Officers, Crew, and Passengers of the Porpoise, upon a small Sand bank near the Wrecks, with sufficient Provisions and Water saved from the Porpoise to subsist the whole, amounting to 80 Men, for Three Months.

Accompanied by the Commander of the Cato, Mr. JOHN PARK, and Twelve Men, I left Wreck Reef in the Cutter with Three Weeks'

Provisions, on Friday, August 26th, in the morning, and on the 28th in the evening made the Land near Indian Head; from whence I kept the coast on board to this place.

I cannot state the Extent of Wreck Reef to the Eastward, but a Bank is visible in that direction six or seven miles from the Wrecks. In a West direction we rowed along the Reef twelve miles, but saw no other dangers in the Passage towards Sandy Cape.--- There are several Passages through the Reef, and Anchorage in from 15 to 22 fathoms upon a sandy bottom, the Flag-staff upon Wreck-reef Bank bearing South-East to South-South-West, distant from three quarters to one-and-quarter mile.

After the above Statement it is unnecessary for me to make Application to Your Excellency to furnish me with the means of Relieving the Crews of the two Ships from the precarious situation in which they are placed, since your Humanity and former unremitting Attention to the Investigator and Porpoise are Sureties that the earliest and most effectual means will be taken, either to bring them back to this Port, or to send them and myself onward towards England.

I inclose to Your Excellency a Letter from Lieut. Fowler upon the occasion; and as he refers to me for the Particulars of the Wreck, an Account thereof is also inclosed. I think it proper to notice to Your

Excellency, that the great exertions of Lieut. Fowler and his Officers, and Company, as well the Passengers belonging to the Investigator in saving His Majesty's Stores, have been very praiseworthy; and I judge that the precautions that were taken will exonerate the Commander of the Porpoise from the blame that might otherwise be attached to the Loss of His Majesty's Armed Vessel.

I have the honour to be
Your Excellency's
Obedient humble Servant,
MATTHEW FLINDERS.

*** We hope to state the Particulars of this untoward Event in our next Week's Paper.

Account of the loss of His Majesty's Armed Vessel Porpoise and the Cato upon Wreck Reef.

[This edited extract from the page 2 account of the shipwreck lists the provisions in the store tent that Trim was responsible for protecting.]

'By the evening of the 23d [August] the whole of the water, and almost the whole of the provisions were landed on the bank, and their stock was now found to consist of the following quantities and proportions for 94 men at full allowance:

Biscuit - 920 | pounds
Flour - 6944 ditto | 83 days
Beef in 4 pounds 1776 pieces |
Pork in 2 pounds 592 ditto | 94 days
Pease - - 45 bushels - 107 days
Oatmeal - 30 ditto - 48 days
Rice - 1225 pounds - 114 days
Sugar - 370 pounds |
Molasses - 125 ditto | 84 days
Spirits - 225 gallons |
Wine - 113 ditto | 49 days
Porter - 60 ditto |
Water, 5650 gallons - 120 days at half-a-gallon per day
With some sour krout, essence of malt, vinegar and salt.

The other stores consisted of a new suit of sails, some whole and some broken spars, iron-work, the armourer's forge, a kedge anchor and hawser, rope, junk, canvas, some twine and other small stores; and four half-barrels of powder, two swivels, and several musquets and pistols, with ball and flints.

Until the 25th [August] they were employed in fitting up the cutter, which was now called the *Hope*, for her expedition, and in still adding to their stock upon the bank: for although the sea had much shaken the ship since the holds were emptied, yet she still stood, and they hoped would keep together at least until the next spring tides.

At Lieutenant Fowler's own request Captain Flinders ordered that he should remain with the stores until the last boat; and that Lieutenant Flinders [Matt's brother Samuel], and Mr. John Aken the master of the *Investigator* should take charge of the two large boats, with a master's mate in each capable of conducting them to Port Jackson, should illness or any accident happen to the two officers.

On Friday the 26th of August in the morning, Captain Flinders and his companions embarked in the cutter, to the number of fourteen, with three weeks provisions. With minds full of hope mixed with anxiety, they returned the three cheers given by their ship-mates on the bank, who immediately hauled down the ensign which had been hitherto hoisted with the union downwards as a signal of distress, and now hoisted the union in the upper canton.'

Incident 10

*'The **Minikin** being very leaky, was obliged to stop at the Isle of France; and there poor Trim, his master and few followers were all made prisoners; under the pretext that they had come to spy out the nakedness of the land; though it was clear as day, that they knew nothing of the war that had taken place a few months before.'*

ACCORDING TO TRIM

The *Cumberland* was not only overrun with rodents (which I tried to deal with), it was also dangerously leaky, with pumps that were so defective that a large part of the day was spent at them to keep the water down. That's why we dropped into Port Louis on 17 December for emergency repairs, a decision that changed our lives. Instead of a warm welcome and thanks for looking after Captain Baudin and the crew of *Le Géographe* in Port Jackson the year before, we were incarcerated for months in a stifling room in a filthy tavern (Café Marengo), where we were besieged by bugs. I did my bit to keep spirits up, but it was challenging.

When Matt was transferred to Maison Despeaux with the other British POWs, I was despatched to the home of a French lady to be her daughter's pet cat. Matt meant well and she was probably a very nice lady, but that's not how I saw my destiny. I'm no 'mincing in amongst cup and saucers' house cat. I'm a ship's cat. I've sailed the world. I've circumnavigated Australia. I've survived a shipwreck. I didn't see myself ending my days on a lap waiting for a pat or the next meal.

That's when I decided that if I couldn't continue exploring the world with Matt, I'd set off on my own and do it. I had no particular plans, but I knew I was perfectly capable of feeding myself and fending for myself, and I had a whole island with a wealth of natural history to observe and examine. So that's what I've done. Who knows, I may even find where the dodos are hiding!

TRIM, THE CARTOGRAPHER'S CAT

Timeline

The Voyages of
Matthew Flinders and Trim

1795

Flinders joins HMS *Reliance* as Master's Mate under the command of Henry Waterhouse, taking Captain John Hunter out to his new job as second governor of the fledgling penal colony of New South Wales.

1796

Reliance sails for Cape Town in September 1797 – Waterhouse had a commission to buy livestock for the colony. Flinders takes the opportunity to sit his lieutenant's exams. Waterhouse stocks up on cattle and merino sheep.

1797

Reliance leaves Cape Town in April bound for Botany Bay. Trim was born on board somewhere in the middle of the Indian Ocean which is why Flinders refers to him as 'Indian by birth' in his Biographical Tribute.

1798

Flinders is promoted to the rank of lieutenant in January and takes command of His Majesty's Sloop *Norfolk* in October to circumnavigate Van Diemen's Land [Tasmania] with George Bass. That's a first. Trim remains on board *Reliance* carrying out pest control and other duties.

1799

Flinders and Trim sail north to Glass-House Bay and Hervey's Bay [Moreton Bay] in *Norfolk*. Flinders was on the lookout for a large river system to explore the interior. No luck. Trim's job was defence of the bread bags.

1800

Flinders and Trim sail to England in *Reliance* by way of Cape Horn and St Helena. Billeted around with friends, Trim discovers the restrictions of hearth and home. Flinders publishes *Observations on the Coasts of Van Diemen's Land, on Bass's Strait and Its Islands, and on Part of the Coasts of New South Wales: intended to accompany the charts of the late discoveries in those countries)* and successfully pitches his plan to complete the investigation of the coasts of Terra Australis.

1801

On 19 January 1801, the Admiralty signs a commission appointing Flinders lieutenant of His Majesty's Sloop *Investigator*. His sailing instructions are to explore in detail, among other places, that part of the south Australian coastline then referred to as 'the Unknown Coast', and to document its flora and fauna. Trim joins him for their second voyage to the South Seas. First stop Madeira, then Cape Town, and finally *Investigator* drops anchor in the sheltered waters of King George's Sound on 8 December.

King George's Sound, view on the peninsula to the north of Peak Head.
William Westall. National Library of Australia.

1802-3

Flinders begins the survey of the southern coast, encounters Nicolas Baudin in the French exploration ship, *Géographe,* at Encounter Bay in April, and sails through the heads at Port Jackson in May. Two months later, he heads north to commence the survey of the east coast, arriving back in Port Jackson on 9 June 1803, having completed the first circumnavigation of Australia, but not the coastal survey – it was called off as *Investigator* was 'found to be rotten' as Flinders puts it.

1803

Flinders and Trim board HMS *Porpoise* on 10 August – Flinders was keen to get to England to organise a replacement ship and complete the coastal survey. Seven days later, they are wrecked on a coral bank in the Great Barrier Reef. Flinders sails back to Port Jackson in the ship's cutter, *Hope,* for help; Trim stays on Wreck Reef maintaining his usual zeal for protecting the provisions.

Flinders and Trim board the *Cumberland* and sail for England. They drop anchor in Port Louis, Mauritius, on 17 December for emergency repairs, and are made prisoners.

1804–1810

In 1804, when Flinders is transferred to Maison Despeaux, Trim is dispatched to the home of a French lady to be her daughter's companion. He disappears shortly afterwards.

In 1809, Flinders records his grief at Trim's loss in his *A Biographical Tribute to the Memory of Trim*. He is released on parole in 1810 and, back in England, publishes *A Voyage to Terra Australis* with accompanying atlas on 18 July 1814. He dies the next day aged 40.

Notes

Matthew Flinders:
Trim's Shipmate and Bedfellow

1. Matthew Flinders, *Private Journal*, p. 150.
2. *Private Journal*, p. 149.
3. Samuel Richardson, letter to Miss Mulso, quoted in Miriam Allott (ed.), *Novelists on the Novel* (London: Routledge and Kegan Paul, 1959), p. 41.
4. George Eliot, quoted in Andrzej Gasiorek, *Post-War British Fiction: Realism and After* (1995), p. 10.
5. Stephen Murray-Smith, 'Introduction', *A Biographical Tribute to the Memory of Trim* by Matthew Flinders (Sydney: John Ferguson; Halstead Press, 1985), p. 5.
6. Matthew Flinders, letter to Ann Flinders, 25 June 1803, in *Personal Letters from an Extraordinary Life*, ed. Paul Brunton (Sydney: Hordern House, 2002), p. 100.
7. Matthew Flinders, Letter to Ann Flinders, 4 November 1804, in Brunton *Personal Letters*, p. 121.
8. Matthew Flinders, Letter to Philip Gidley King, 24 September 1803, in Brunton *Personal Letters*, pp. 109–110.

9. Murray-Smith, 'Introduction', p. 5.
10. George Gordon McCrae, 'Historical Sketch of Captain Matthew Flinders', *Victorian Geographical Journal*, 28 (1911), p. 13.
11. Matthew Flinders Memorial Statue website (http://www.flindersmemorial.org/the-matthew-flinders-memorial-statue/).

My Seafurring Adventures
with Matt Flinders

Incident 1

12. Henry Waterhouse, letter to Viscount Sydney, 20
August 1797, sold at Christies, London, 29 April
1999 (https://www.christies.com/lotfinder/Lot/
captain-henry-waterhouse-rn-1770-1812-1657199-
details.aspx).

Incident 2

13. James Cook, Journal, 6 May 1770, from *James
Cook: The Journals*, selected and edited by Philip
Edwards (London: Penguin Books, 2003), p. 128.
14. Matthew Flinders, 'Memoir Explaining the
Construction of the Charts of Australia,' TNA
ADM 55/76/36–88, quoted in Dany Bréelle,
'Matthew Flinders's Australian Toponymy and
its British Connections,' Journal of the Hakluyt
Society, November 2013 (https://www.hakluyt.com/
PDF/Flinders_Toponymy.pdf).

Incident 3

15. *Matthew Flinders, A Voyage to Terra Australis in the Years 1801–1803, Volume 1* (London: Nicol, 1814), p. 36.

Incident 6

16. Ken Shilling and Cynthia Hunter, Huntington's History of Newcastle and the Northern District (Lambton, NSW: Newcastle Family History Society, 2009), quoted in 'Seizure of the Norfolk' (https://www.jenwilletts.com/seizure_of_the_norfolk.htm).

17. William Burney (editor), *A New Universal Dictionary of the Marine* (T. Cadell and W. Davies, London 1815).

Incident 7

18. 'the Country itself, so far as we know': James Cook, Journal, 6 May 1770, from *James Cook: The Journals*, selected and edited by Philip Edwards (London: Penguin Books, 2003), p. 175.

Acknowledgements

This book owes its existence to Matthew Flinders RN, who put pen to paper when detained in Plaines Wilhems, Mauritius, and turned his sadness at the loss of 'the most affectionate of friends, – faithful of servants, and best of creatures' into an utterly timeless tale of a ship's cat – *A Biographical Tribute to the Memory of Trim*. We are most grateful to Lisette Flinders Petrie for giving us her permission to embark on this new edition based on our complete and faithful transcript of the six-page manuscript safely lodged in the National Maritime Museum at Greenwich. We would also like to thank Nigel Rigby for his support and for helping us navigate the permissions hoops at the museum, and Helen Whitington, who meticulously checked our transcript.

We always knew that in illustrating *Trim, The Cartographer's Cat* we wanted to make the most of the treasure trove of drawings made by the *Investigator* artists during the circumnavigation of Australia. We also knew we would need more than that, so we turned to Ad Long, who took our briefest of briefs and created delightful images that complement the drawings of the *Investigator* artists perfectly. Of course, that would not have been possible without the ever-patient Fynne, who took time out from his busy feline schedule to be Trim's body double, or without his human,

Nicola Beveridge, who carried out numerous photo shoots.

When we decided we wanted a map that showed Flinders' and Trim's circumnavigation of Australia and other explorations, we turned to John Frith of Flat Earth Mapping, who not only recreated Flinders' map and added in the extra voyages and place names we requested, but helpfully delivered more than we were looking for.

We would like to thank Mark Richards, who generously sent us the photographs of his Flinders and Trim sculpture which is installed in three places – at Euston Station in London, at Flinders University, Adelaide, and in Port Lincoln in South Australia. Interestingly, three is the limit set by Mark regarding the number of copies of the sculpture allowed – there won't be any more.

We didn't solve the mystery of when or where George Gordon McRae read *A Biographical Tribute to the Memory of Trim*, which inspired him to draw 'Trim's short cut, glass all smashed to "Flinders"'. But Dr Rosemary Richards (who has written about Georgiana McRae, his mother) and the State Library of Victoria staff were enormously helpful in our quest.

Jenny Clark, Commissioning Editor at Adlard Coles Nautical (an imprint of Bloomsbury Publishing Plc), immediately got what we were trying to do with our Flinders and Trim manuscript and wanted it. Thank you. And thank you for giving us such a great editorial and production team to bring the book to life:

... bringing the book to life:

our Managing Editors, Jonathan Eyers and
Oonagh Wade, kept us on track.

our Designer, Lee-May Lim,
created pages we wanted to turn.

as for Cover Designer, Sutchinda Thompson,
she got it. In one.

Publishing needs people who make it happen.
Thank you to Rachel Murphy and Brett Rogers.

Books need people to know they are out there on the shelves.
That's where Marketing and Publicity come into the picture
and Alice Graham has been awesome.

Picture Credits

Page 33

Augustus Earle, c.1826. *Portrait of Bungaree, a native of New South Wales, with Fort Macquarie, Sydney Harbour, in background.* National Library of Australia. PIC T305. NK118.

Page 35

Ferdinand Bauer. Cheilopogon sp., *flyingfish.* Plate 37 from Zoological drawings. Natural History Museum, London. ALM-DTF762.

Page 37

George Gordon McCrae, c.1860. *Trim's short cut, glass all smashed to 'Flinders'.* National Library of Australia. PIC Volume 1008 #R8203.

Page 40

William Westall, 1814. *View in Sir Edward Pellew's group, Gulph* [sic] *of Carpentaria*; engraved by John Pye. National Library of Australia. PIC Solander Box B31 #S2276.

Page 45

William Westall, 1802. *Wreck of the* Porpoise, *Flinders expedition.* National Library of Australia. PIC Solander box B30 #R7062.

Page 55

Toussaint Antoine de Chazal de Chamarel, Mauritius, 1806–1807. *Portrait of Captain Matthew Flinders, RN, 1774-1814.* Art Gallery of South Australia. 20005P22.

Page 61

George Gordon McCrae, c.1860. *Matthew Flinders, Capt. R.N. 1809, Author of Trim.* National Library of Australia. PIC Volume 1008 #R8205.

Page 63
Mark Richards, 2014. Statue of Matthew Flinders and Trim, Euston Station, London. Photo courtesy Mark Richards.

Page 73
Samuel Calvert, 1865. *Captain Cook taking possession of the Australian Continent on behalf of the British Crown, 1770, under the name of New South Wales.* National Library of Australia. PIC Solander Box B7 # 54632.

Page 76
William Westall, 1814. *View of Port Jackson taken from the South Head*; engraved by John Pye. National Library of Australia. PIC Solander Box B31 #S2275.

Page 97
William Westall, 1802. *Thistle Island: a snake.* National Library of Australia. PIC Solander Box B17 #R4272.

Page 101
William Westall, 1803. *View of Wreck Reef bank taken at low water, Terra Australis.* National Library of Australia. Rex Nan Kivell Collection NK9938.

Page 114
William Westall, 1801. *King George's Sound, view on the peninsula to the north of Peak Head.* National Library of Australia. PIC Solander Box B16 # R4265.

About the Authors

'I have too much ambition to rest in the unnoticed middle order of mankind, and since neither birth nor fortune have favoured me, my actions shall speak to the world.' They certainly did. **Matthew Flinders RN** (16 March 1774 – 19 July 1814), one of the world's most accomplished navigators and cartographers, was the first to circumnavigate Australia and was the man who gave the continent its name. His *A Voyage to Terra Australis*, with an accompanying atlas (2 vols) was published on 18 July 1814. It had taken him four years to complete it. He died the next day at forty years of age. He also contributed to the science of navigation, including carrying out research on tide action and on compass deviation due to the presence of iron in ships. Ill health, homesickness and loneliness did not deter him from his focus on his goals. In *A Biographical Tribute to the Memory of Trim,* he transforms his grief over the loss of his beloved seafurrer shipmate who sailed with him for many years into the world's most timeless tale about a ship's cat.

Editor, writer, singer, librarian and other stuff like that, **Gillian Dooley PhD** is an Honorary Senior Research Fellow at Flinders University, South Australia. She has published widely on various literary and historical topics, often with a particular emphasis on music. When not hard at work cataloguing every dance and ditty in Jane Austen's personal music collection or editing books on the philosophy of Iris Murdoch or the novels of Rabindranath Tagore, she is an inveterate conference traveller: in 2018 alone she gave presentations in Hyderabad, Kyoto, Kuala Lumpur, Mauritius, Sri Lanka, Parramatta, Adelaide and Perth. She has published two monographs and several scholarly editions, including *Matthew Flinders' Private Journal 1803–1814*, and in 2014 presented the Royal Society Matthew Flinders Memorial Lecture at the Royal Society of Victoria to mark the bicentenary of Matthew's untimely death.

Philippa Sandall is a writer and the founding editor of the online health newsletter GI News, which, with Alan Barclay and Jennie Brand-Miller, she has built up to have 100,000 subscribers worldwide. Of the numerous books she has co-authored, her favourites are: *Sticks, Seeds, Pods & Leaves* (Hardie Grant), *Recipes My Mother Cooked* (Allen & Unwin), *The Ultimate Guide to Sugars & Sweeteners* (The Experiment) and *The Good Carbs Cookbook* (Allen & Unwin). She sailed solo with *Seafurrers: The Ships' Cats Who Lapped and Mapped the World* (The Experiment). The essential ABCs of her life include family and friends, taking a walk on the beach, writing, history and her Seafurrers website (www.seafurrers.com), which she has fun working on with Ky Long (designer) and Ad Long (illustrator), fuelled by regular team catch-ups over coffee at Gertrude & Alice café/bookstore, Bondi Beach.

Index